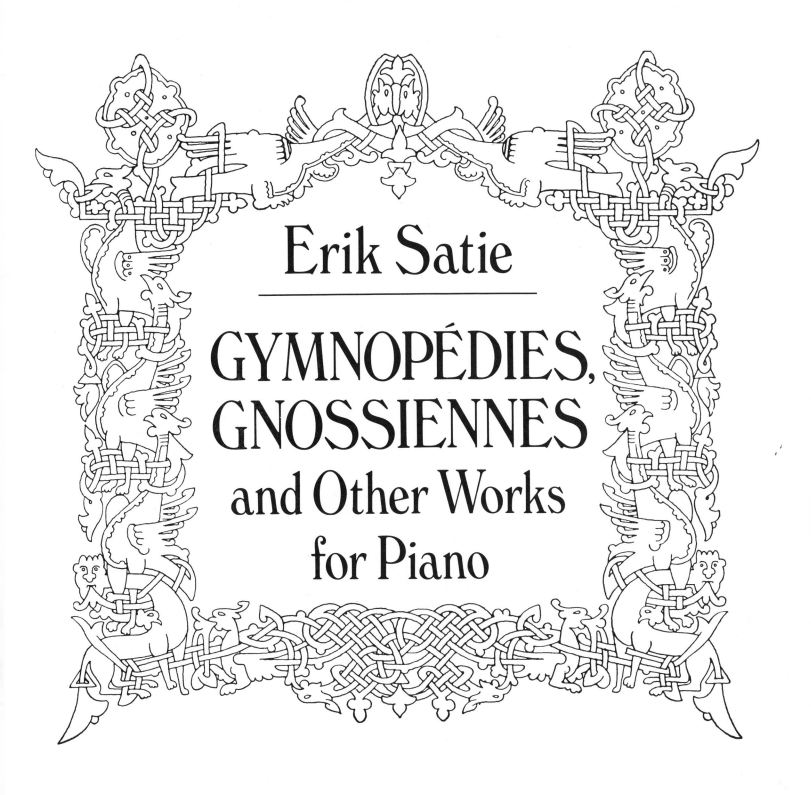

Erik Satie

GYMNOPÉDIES, GNOSSIENNES

and Other Works for Piano

Dover Publications, Inc., New York

D1206347

Published in Canada by General Publishing Company, Ltd., 30 Lesmill Road, Don Mills, Toronto, Ontario.
Published in the United Kingdom by Constable and Company, Ltd.

This Dover edition, first published in 1989, is a new collection of works, reproduced from the following editions:

Sarabandes, Rouart, Lerolle & Cie, Paris, [1887]; *Gymnopédies,* Rouart, Lerolle, [1888]; *Trois Gnossiennes,* Rouart, Lerolle, 1913; *Le Fils des Etoiles: Wagnérie Kaldéenne du Sar Peladan,* Rouart, Lerolle, [1891]; *Sonneries de la Rose + Croix,* Rouart, Lerolle, 1892; *Prélude de La Porte Héroïque du Ciel,* Rouart, Lerolle, 1912; *Pièces Froides,* Rouart, Lerolle, 1912; *Poudre d'Or,* Rouart, Lerolle, n.d.; *3 Morceaux en forme de Poire (à 4 mains) avec une Manière de Commencement, une Prolongation du même & un En Plus, suivi d'une Redite,* Rouart, Lerolle, 1911; *En Habit de Cheval,* Rouart, Lerolle, 1911; *Aperçus désagréables,* E. Demets, 1913; *Véritables Préludes Flasques (pour un Chien),* E. Demets, 1912; *Descriptions Automatiques,* E. Demets, 1913; *Embryons desséchés,* E. Demets, 1913; *Croquis et Agaceries d'un gros Bonhomme en bois,* E. Demets, 1913; *Chapitres tournés en tous sens,* E. Demets, 1913; *Vieux Sequins et vieilles Cuirasses,* E. Demets, 1913.

The titles and directions have been newly translated by Stanley Appelbaum, and a table of contents has been added.

Manufactured in the United States of America
Dover Publications, Inc., 31 East 2nd Street, Mineola, N.Y. 11501

Library of Congress Cataloging-in-Publication Data

Satie, Erik, 1866–1925.
  [Piano music. Selections]
  Gymnopédies, Gnossiennes and other works for piano.

  Works 9–11 for piano, 4 hands.
  Reprint of works originally published 1887–1913.
  Contents: Sarabandes—Gymnopédies—Trois gnossiennes—[etc.]
  1. Piano music.   2. Piano music (4 hands)   I. Title.
M22.S25D7   1989   89-751232
ISBN 0-486-25978-1

CONTENTS

NOTE ON THE TRANSLATIONS

Except for long epigraphs, which are placed high on the page, all the translations appear
at the foot of the respective page, run on, in the order of the appearance of the French (or
Latin, Spanish, . . .) words on the page. With a few intentional exceptions, a single
French (etc.) term is translated only once within a given piece. Standard Italian musical
terms are not translated.

1ᴱᴿᴱ SARABANDE

Septembre 1887

1ST SARABANDE (September 1887).

Rallentando.

2ᵉᵐᵉ SARABANDE

Septembre 1887

à Maurice RAVEL

2ND SARABANDE (September 1887). Diminuendo. Rallentando.

3ᴱᴹᴱ SARABANDE

Septembre 1887

3RD SARABANDE (September 1887).

1.ère GYMNOPÉDIE

1ST GYMNOPAIDIKE [Spartan dance of naked youths and men]. Slow and sorrowful.

à CONRAD SATIE

2.ème GYMNOPÈDIE

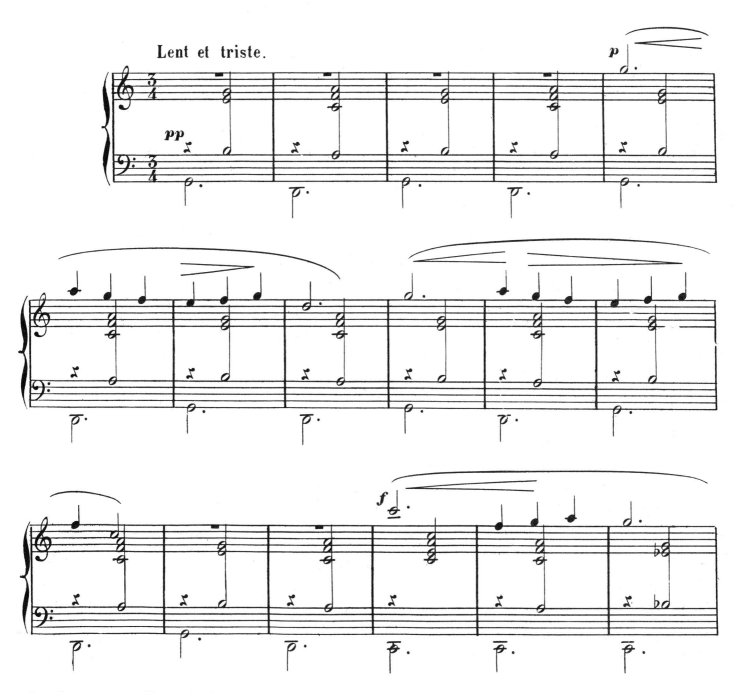

2ND GYMNOPAIDIKE. Slow and sad.

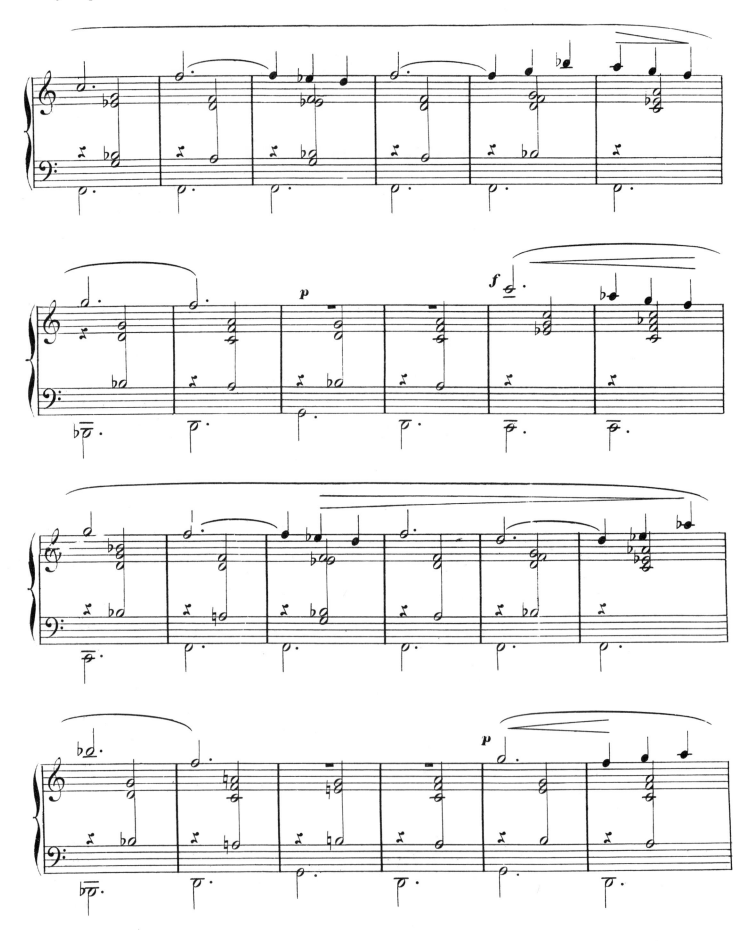

3.ᵐᵉ GYMNOPÉDIE

Lent et grave.

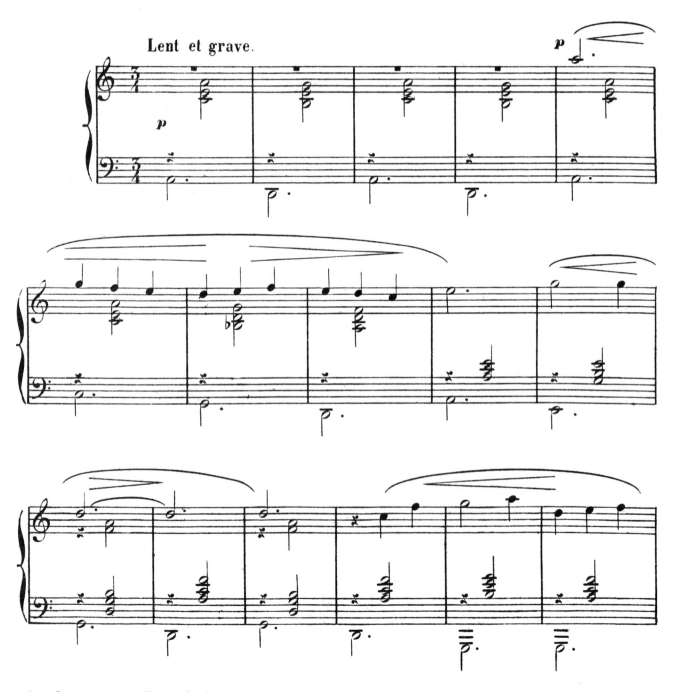

3RD GYMNOPAIDIKE. Slow and solemn.

GNOSSIENNE

(1890)

à Roland MANUEL

№ 1

GNOSSIENNE [Dance of ancient Knosos, Crete (?)] (1890). Slow. Very shiny. Ask.

Du bout de la pensée

Postulez en vous-même

Pas u Pas

Sur la langue

With the tip of your thought. Postulate within yourself. Step by step. On the tongue.

GNOSSIENNE

(1890)

№ 2

GNOSSIENNE (1890). With surprise. Don't go out. With great kindness.

More intimately. With slight intimacy. Without pridefulness.

GNOSSIENNE

(1890)

№ 3

GNOSSIENNE (1890). Slow. Advise yourself carefully. Arm yourself with clairvoyance. Alone for an instant. So that you obtain a hollow.

Tres perdu

Portez cela plus loin

Ouvrez la tête

Enfouissez le son

Very lost. Carry that further. Open your head. Bury the sound.

LE FILS DES ÉTOILES

Wagnérie Kaldéenue du Sar PÉLADAN

Dédication: Sans préjudice des pratiques des grands imprécateurs Mes cousins, J'offre cette œuvre à Mes pairs. Par ainsi, et pour la précédence des exemples, Je ne demande point l'exaltation. J'appelle sur Mes convives la miséricorde du Père, créateur des choses visibles et invisibles; la protection de la Mère Auguste du Rédempteur, Reine des Anges; comme les prières du chœur glorieux des Apôtres et des Saints Ordres des Esprits bienheureux. Que la juste inflammation de Dieu écrase les superbes et les indécents! — Erik Satie

Dedication: Without prejudice to the practices of the great imprecators My cousins, I offer this work to my peers. Thus, and for the precedence of the examples, I do not ask for exaltation. I call down upon My guests-at-table the mercy of the Father, creator of things visible and invisible; the protection of the August Mother of the Redeemer, Queen of Angels; as well as the prayers of the glorious chorus of the Apostles and the Holy Orders of blessed Spirits. May the just choler of God crush the haughty and the indecent! — Erik Satie

PRÉLUDE DU 1er ACTE — LA VOCATION

Thème décoratif : *La nuit de Kaldée*

THE SON OF THE STARS. A CHALDEAN WAGNERY BY SÂR PÉLADAN. PRELUDE TO THE 1ST ACT: THE CALLING. Decorative theme: The Night of Chaldea. In white and motionless. Still [in the same manner]. With preciosity. Pale and hieratic.

Comme une douce demande.

Toujours.

Précieusement.

Pâle et hiératique.

Like a gentle request. Still [in the same manner]. With preciosity.

Prélude du 2ᵉ Acte — L'Initiation

Thème décoratif: *La salle basse du Grand Temple*

PRELUDE TO THE 2ND ACT: THE INITIATION. Decorative theme: The lower hall of the Great Temple. In your
head. Less high. Rising. Courageously easy and complaisantly solitary. The same. With preciosity.

Tomber jusqu'à l'affaiblissement.

Courageusement facile et complaisamment solitaire.

De même

Toujours

Précieusement   Toujours

Fall to the point of weakness. Still [in the same manner].

PRÉLUDE DU 3ᵉ ACTE — L'INCANTATION

Thème décoratif: *La terrasse du palais du patesi GOUDÉA*

PRELUDE TO THE 3RD ACT: THE INCANTATION. Decorative theme: The terrace of the palace of the patesi [Sumerian ruler] Gudea. Very good. Still [in the same manner]. Looking at oneself from afar. Very good. The same.

Without shuddering too much. Be closer. Still [in the same manner]. Looking at oneself from afar. To ignore one's own presence. High.

Rising. Very good. In your head. The same. Without becoming irritated. Finish for oneself. Still [in the same manner].

SONNERIES DE LA ROSE + CROIX

AIR DE L'ORDRE

TRUMPET CALLS OF THE ROSE + CROSS [this is the piano version of a work for trumpets and harps]. THEME OF THE ORDER. Slow and nonlegato without dryness.

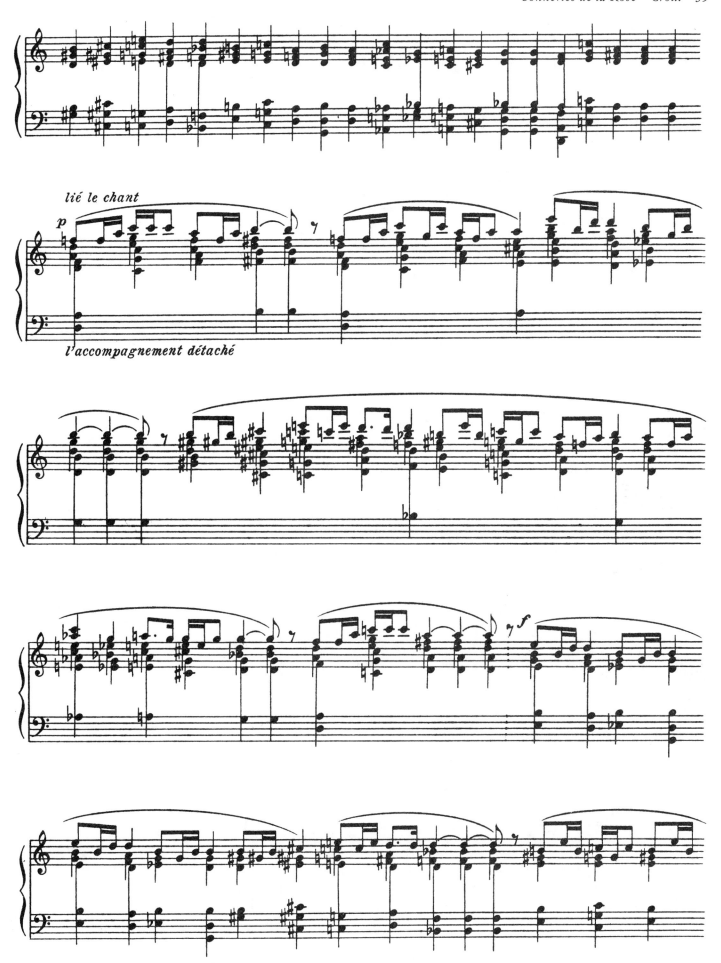

The melody legato. The accompaniment nonlegato.

SONNERIES DE LA ROSE + CROIX

AIR DU GRAND MAITRE

Le Sâr JOSÉPHIN PÉLADAN

THEME OF THE GRAND MASTER. Slow. Nonlegato without dryness.

The melody legato. The accompaniment nonlegato.

SONNERIES DE LA ROSE+CROIX

AIR DU GRAND PRIEUR

Le Comte ANTOINE de La ROCHEFOUCAULD

THEME OF THE GRAND PRIOR. Nonlegato. Slow. Legato.

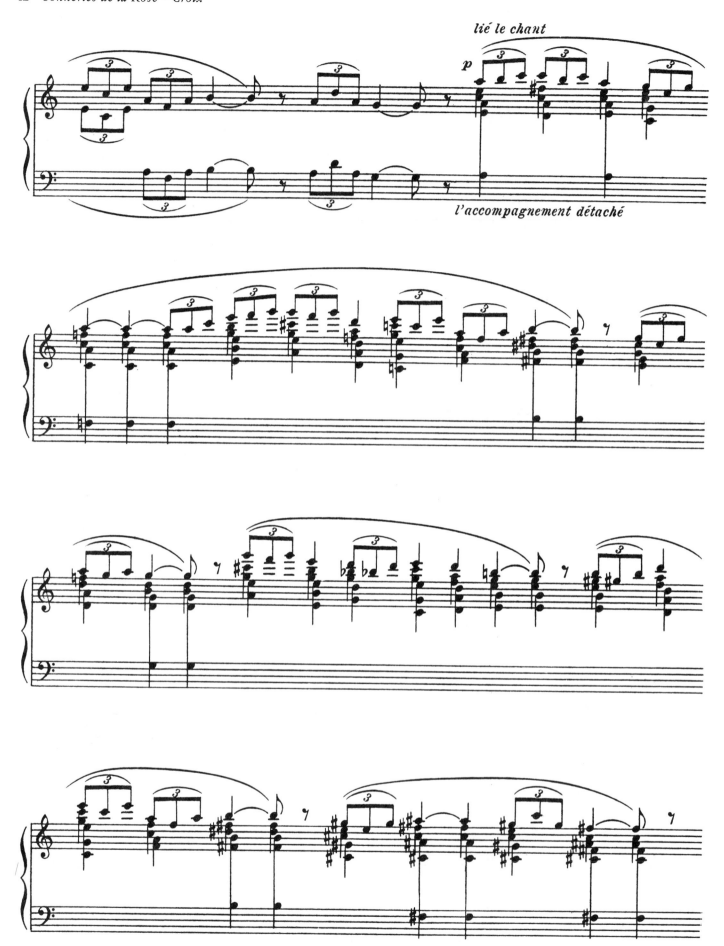

The melody legato. The accompaniment nonlegato.

PRÉLUDE DE LA PORTE HÉROÏQUE DU CIEL

(1894)

Je me dédie cette œuvre. E. S.

Drame ésotérique de
JULES BOIS

Musique de
ERIK SATIE

PRELUDE TO THE HEROIC GATE OF HEAVEN. I dedicate this work to myself, E. S. Esoteric drama by Jules Bois, music by Erik Satie. Calm and profoundly tender. Superstitiously. With deference. Very sincerely silent.

With timid piety. Avoid all sacrilegious exaltation. Without pridefulness. Obligingly. Curtain.

PIÈCES FROIDES
(1897)

Airs à faire fuir

a RICARDO VIÑÉS

I

COLD PIECES (1897). MELODIES THAT SCARE YOU AWAY. In a very particular manner. Obey.

Complete. Descend. Become fixed. Don't torment yourself.

Weary. Important. Enigmatic. Aside. At bottom.

II

With fascination. Farther away. Pure. Modestly. Without frowning.

A sucer

Dans le plus profond silence

To be sucked. In the profoundest silence.

III

Invite yourself. Don't eat too much. Cumulatively.

Dernièrement

Lastly.

See. Don't eat too much. Good.

PIÈCES FROIDES
(1897)

Danses de travers

à Madame J. ECORCHEVILLE

I

En y regardant à deux fois

Se le dire

COLD PIECES (1897). CROOKED DANCES. Considering carefully in advance. Tell yourself.

Flat. White. Still [in the same manner].

II

Pass. Similarly. With the corner of the hand.

Alone. Be visible a moment. Fit together. Somewhat cooked.

III

Again. Better. Again.

Very good. Marvelous.

Perfect. Don't go any higher. Without noise. Very distant.

POUDRE D'OR

VALSE

GOLD DUST. WALTZ. Moderato. The melody very prominent.

Ritenuto.

Languorously. Brightly.

MORCEAUX EN FORME DE POIRE

(Septembre 1903)

Manière de Commencement

PIECES IN PEAR FORM (September 1903). BY WAY OF A BEGINNING. Proceed moderately. With a great deal of care. A bit livelier.

MORCEAUX EN FORME DE POIRE

(Septembre 1903)

Manière de Commencement[1]

PRIMA

(1) "Gnossienne" extraite du *Fils des Etoiles* 1891.

The melody prominent. (1) This "Gnossienne" is an excerpt from *Le fils des étoiles*, 1891.

Rallentando. Dryly.

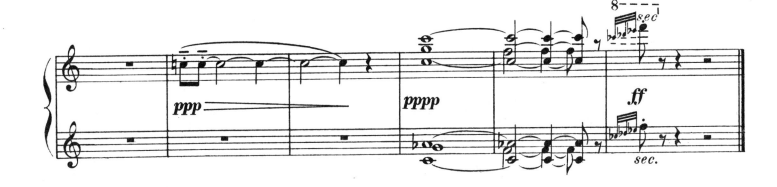

Prolongation du même

SECONDA

Au pas

EXTENSION OF THE SAME. At a walking pace. Lightly. More broadly. Rallentando.

Prolongation du même

PRIMA

Ritenuto.

I

SECONDA

Slowly. Rallentando.

I

PRIMA

Prominently. The hand lowered.

en dehors
la main abaissée

II

SECONDA

Con brio. Rallentando.

II

PRIMA

De moitié

At half the preceding tempo.

Ritenuto.

Premier temps

Tempo primo. Rallentando.

Premier temps

III

SECONDA

Brutally. Espressivo. Lightly. Cantabile. Ritenuto.

III

PRIMA

Moderato.

Like an animal. With suppleness.

SECONDA

Rallentando. A tempo.

Crescendo (?). Dryly.

En plus

SECONDA

IN ADDITION. Tranquillo. Of the same color.

En plus

PRIMA

la main très abaissée

The hand very low.

SECONDA

Rallentando.

Redite

SECONDA

REPETITION. On the slow side. Cantabile. Lightly. Diminuendo e ritenuto.

Redite

PRIMA

Both hands together. With both hands.

EN HABIT DE CHEVAL

(Juin - Aout 1911)

Choral

SECUNDUS

Fugue Litanique

IN RIDING HABIT (June–August 1911). CHORALE. Weighty—very. With preciosity. Heavy. Rallentando. Swell. LITANY-FUGUE. Carefully and slowly.

EN HABIT DE CHEVAL

(Juin - Aout 1911)

Choral

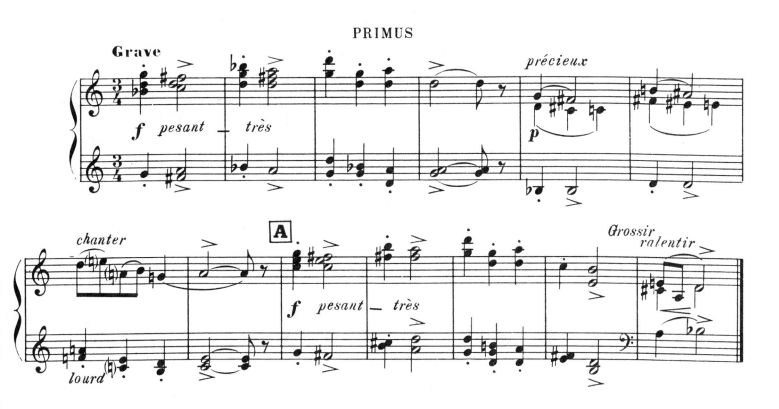

Fugue Litanique

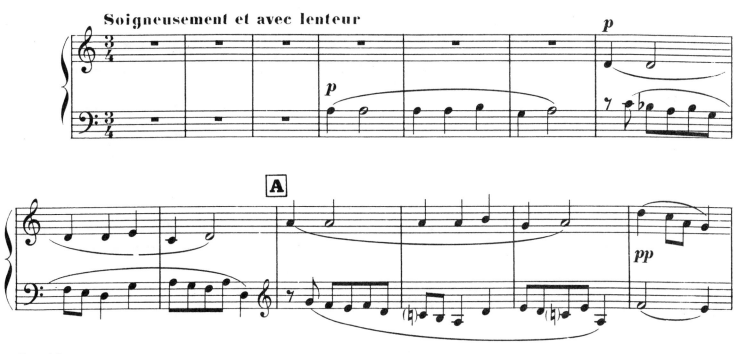

Cantabile.

Espressivo.

Autre Choral

ANOTHER CHORALE. Not slowly. Cantabile. Rallentando.

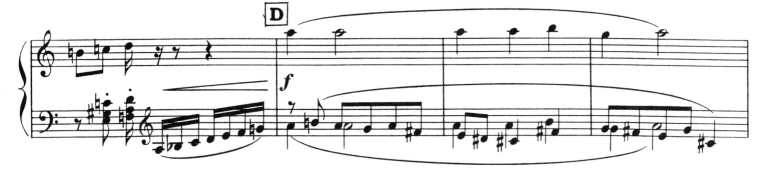

Autre Choral

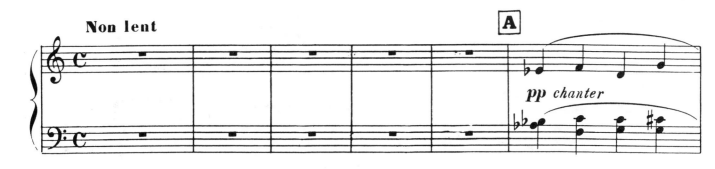

Fugue de Papier

PAPER FUGUE. Quite moderate.

Fugue de Papier

Assez modéré

la main en dessous

Right hand under.

More slowly. Rallentando.

Even more.

APERÇUS DÉSAGRÉABLES

PASTORALE, CHORAL et FUGUE

(Septembre 1908 - Octobre 1912)

PASTORALE

UNPLEASANT OBSERVATIONS: PASTORALE, CHORALE AND FUGUE (September 1908–October 1912). PASTORALE. Quite slow.

APERÇUS DÉSAGRÉABLES

PASTORALE, CHORAL et FUGUE

(Septembre 1908 - Octobre 1912)

PASTORALE

Very legato and melancholy. See. Lightly but strongly.

Rallentando. Resume. With swelling sound. Ritenuto, please. Slower. Prominently.

Particularly.

CHORAL

CHORALE. Broadminded. Don't turn. Very cantabile. Better. Again. Scratch.

CHORAL

Positively.

FUGUE

FUGUE. Not fast. Smile. Ever since. Prominently.

FUGUE

With pleasure. Naturally.

Straight. Visible. Take. Necessarily.

Without spite. In a corner. Cantabile. Much.

Don't talk. With preciosity. Look. Genuine. Ritenuto. Nobly.

Remains to be seen. Say. Alone. Facing.

VÉRITABLES
PRÉLUDES FLASQUES

(pour un chien)

Très "neuf heures du matin"
Ricardo Viñes

GENUINE FLABBY PRELUDES (FOR A DOG). Very "nine in the morning"—Ricardo Viñes. SEVERE REPRIMAND. Lively (but not too). Give. The same. Drunk. Convince.

Imbiber

Corpulentus

Cæremoniosus

Pædagogus
Retenir

En force

12 Août 1912

Imbibe. Corpulent. Ceremonious. Pedagogue. Ritenuto. In full force. August 12, 1912.

ALONE AT HOME. Gently. With sadness. Nocturnal. Illusory. Substantial. Attentively. Ritenuto e cantabile. August 17, 1912.

ON JOUE

SOMEONE IS PLAYING. Go. Legato. A bit. Resume. Opaque. Imitative.

Sudden. Separate [Broaden?]. August 23, 1912.

23 Août 1912

DESCRIPTIONS
AUTOMATIQUES

SUR UN VAISSEAU

Au gré des flots

Assez lent

Léger

Petit embrun   Un autre

Coup d'air frais   Mélancolie maritime

Petit embrun

AUTOMATIC DESCRIPTIONS. ON A BOAT. Drifting with the Current. Quite slow. l.h. Lightly. A small dash of spray. Another. A gust of cool air. Melancholy at sea. A small dash of spray.

126

Un nouveau

Gentil tangage

Petite lame

Le capitaine dit: Très beau voyage

Le vaisseau ricane

Liez

Paysage au loin

Yet another one. Mild pitching. A small wave. The captain says: "A very fine voyage." The boat gives a nasty laugh. Legato. Landscape in the distance.

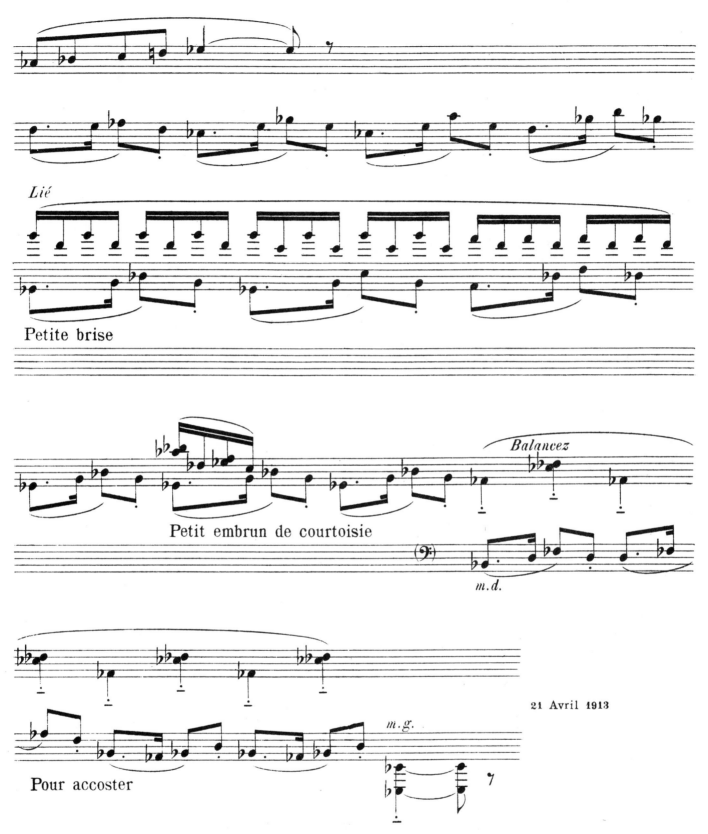

Lié

Petite brise

Balancez

Petit embrun de courtoisie

m.d.

21 Avril 1913

m.g.

Pour accoster

A light breeze. A small complimentary dash of spray. r.h. With a rocking motion. In order to come alongside. April 21, 1913.

à Madame Joseph RAVEL

SUR UNE LANTERNE

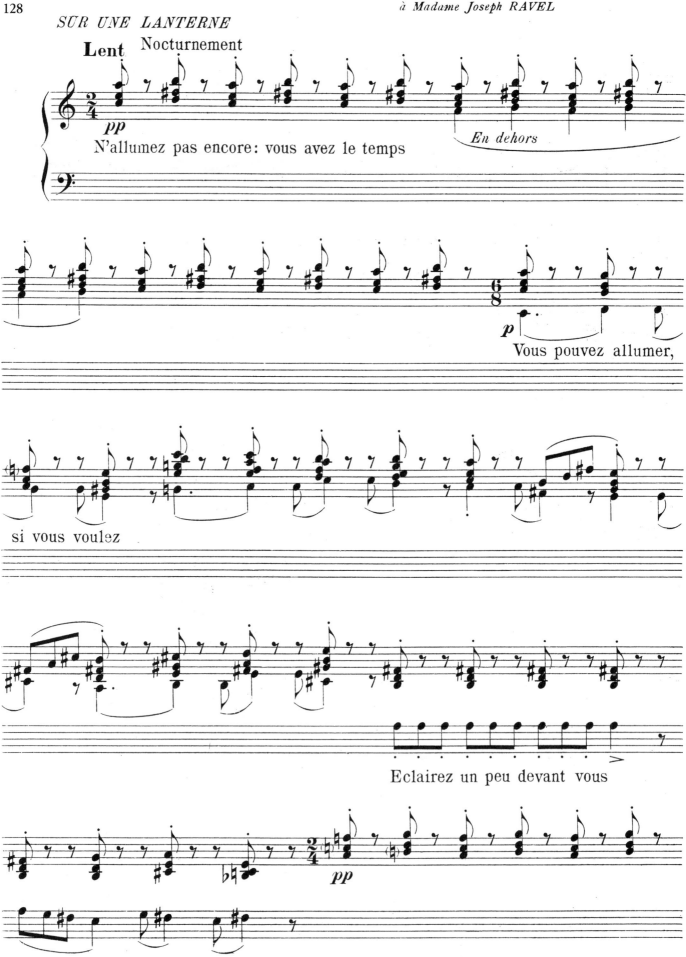

ON A LANTERN. Slow. Nocturnally. Don't turn on the light yet: you have time. Prominently. You can turn on the light if you like.
Flash the light in front of you.

Your hand shielding the light. Withdraw your hand and put it in your pocket.

Pressez un peu

f *p*

f Elargissez *Retenir et diminuer*

pp

Chut! Attendez
(deux temps) Eteignez

Ecartez

22 Avril 1913

With a little more urgency. More broadly. Ritenuto e diminuendo. Sh! Wait (two beats). Turn off the light. Separate [Broaden?]. April 22, 1913.

ON A HELMET. Quick step. They arrive. So many people! Demolished mechanism (OR: technique). It's wonderful! Here come the drummers!

That fine-looking man all by himself is the colonel. Heavy as a sow. Light as an egg. Slight ritenuto. Dryly. April 26, 1913.

EMBRYONS DESSÉCHÉS

à Mademoiselle Suzanne ROUX

I d'Holothurie

Ignorant people call it "sea cucumber."

The HOLOTHURIAN usually climbs up rocks or blocks of stone.

Like the cat, this sea animal purrs; moreover, it spins dripping threads of silk.

The action of light seems to disturb it.

I observed a Holothurian in the Gulf of Saint-Malo [between Normandy and Brittany].

Les ignorants l'appellent le "*concombre des mers*".

L'HOLOTHURIE grimpe ordinairement sur des pierres ou des quartiers de roche.

Comme le chat, cet animal marin ronronne; de plus, il file une soie dégouttante.

L'action de la lumière semble l'incommoder.

J'observai une Holothurie dans la baie de Saint-Malo.

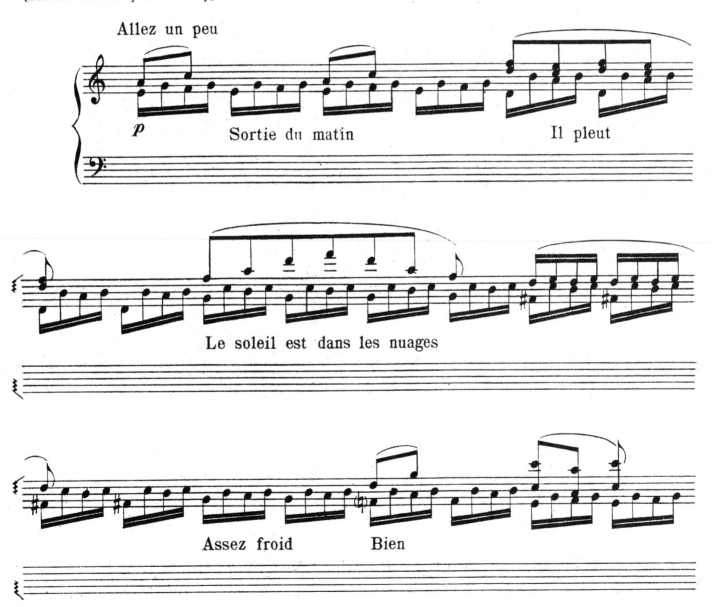

DRIED EMBRYOS. I: OF A HOLOTHURIAN. Walk a bit. Going out in the morning. It's raining. The sun is behind clouds. Pretty cold. All right.

Little purr. What a pretty boulder! Life is wonderful.

Ritenuto. Rallentando molto. Like a nightingale with a toothache. A tempo. Returning home in the evening. It's raining.

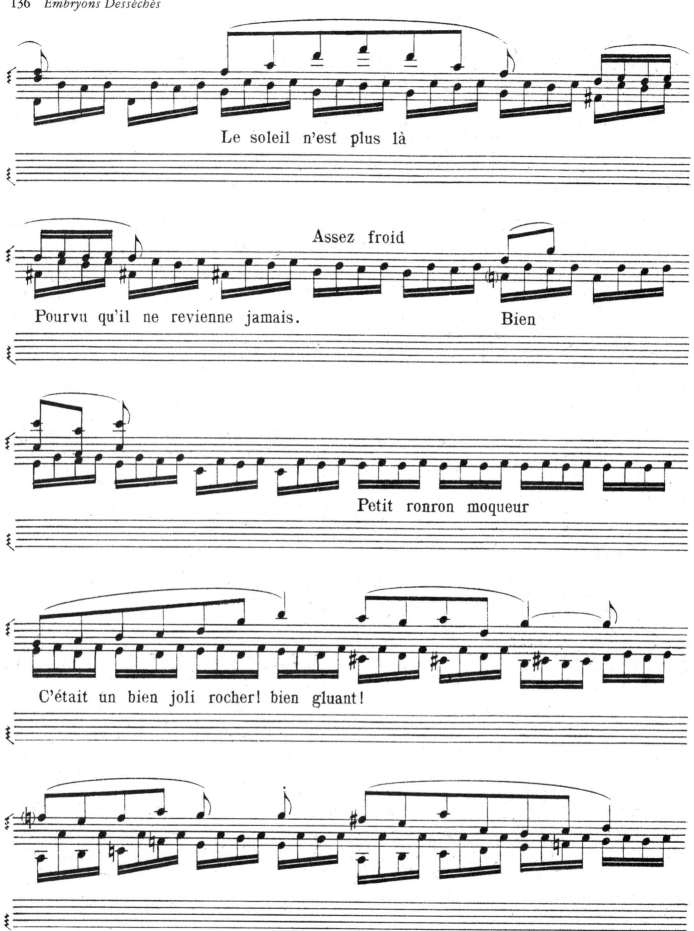

Le soleil n'est plus là

Pourvu qu'il ne revienne jamais.   Assez froid   Bien

Petit ronron moqueur

C'était un bien joli rocher! bien gluant!

The sun is gone. I hope it never comes back. Pretty cold. All right. Little sarcastic purr. It was a really pretty boulder! Nice and sticky!

Don't make me laugh, sprig of moss: You're tickling me. I have no tobacco. Good thing I don't smoke. Grandiose. The best you can do. June 30, 1913.

à Monsieur Edouard DREYFUS

II d'Edriophthalma

Crustaceans with sessile eyes, that is, stalkless, immobile eyes. Very melancholy by nature, these crustaceans live apart from society in holes drilled through cliffs.

Crustacés à yeux sessiles, c'est-à-dire sans tige et immobiles. Très tristes de leur naturel, ces crustacés vivent, retirés du monde, dans des trous percés à travers les falaises.

II. OF AN EDRIOPHTHALMA. Somber. They are all assembled. How sad it is! A father of a family starts to speak. They all start crying (quotation from the famous mazurka by Schubert).

Pauvres bêtes!

Ralentir *pp* Comme il a bien parlé! *p*

f Grand gémissement.

pp *Retenir beaucoup*

1 Juillet 1913

Poor animals! Rallentando. How well he spoke! A great moaning. Ritenuto molto. July 1, 1913.

à Madame Jane MORTIER

III de Podophthalma

Crustaceans with eyes placed on movable stalks. They are skillful and tireless hunters. They are found in all the oceans. The flesh of the Podophthalma is tasty food.

Crustacés à yeux placés sur des tiges mobiles. Ce sont d'adroits, d'infatigables chasseurs. On les rencontre dans toutes les mers. La chair du Podophthalma constitue une savoureuse nourriture.

III: OF A PODOPHTHALMA. Fairly brisk. Out hunting. Mount. Pursuit.

An adviser. He's right! Pause. Slower. In order to cast a spell over the game. Rallentando.

142

Reprendre en augmentant peu à peu le mouvement

Qu'est-ce?

Le conseilleur

Resume, getting gradually faster. What is it? The adviser.

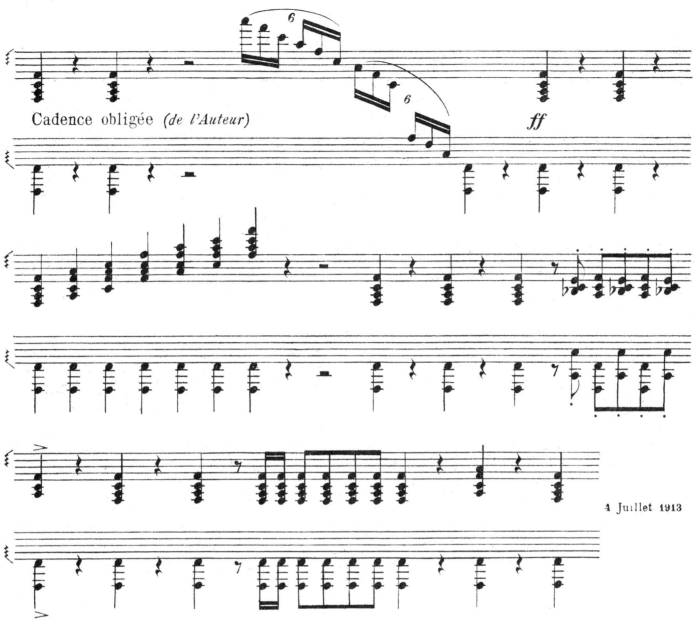

Cadence obligée *(de l'Auteur)*

ff

4 Juillet 1913

Obligatory cadenza (by the composer). July 4, 1913.

CROQUIS & AGACERIES D'UN
GROS BONHOMME EN BOIS

à Mademoiselle Elvira VIÑES SOTO

Nº 1 _ Tyrolienne turque.

Avec précaution et lent

Dans le gosier

Un peu chaud

SKETCHES & PROVOCATIONS OF A PORTLY WOODEN MANNIKIN. NO. 1: TURKISH YODEL SONG. With precaution and slowly. Down in the throat. A little warm.

Du bout des yeux et retenu d'avance

Beaucoup d'expression et plus lent

Très turc

With the tip of the eyes and held back in advance. With much expression and more slowly. Very Turkish.

Impassible

Encore

Reprendre

peu saignant

retardez

28 Juillet 1913

Impassive. Resume. Again. Just a bit rare (OR: bleeding). Ritardando. July 28, 1913.

à Monsieur Hernando VINĒS SOTO

Nᵒ 2_ *Danse maigre* *(à la manière de ces messieurs)*

No. 2: Thin (or: Lenten) Dance (in the style of "their Lordships"). Fairly slow, if you don't mind. Distant and bored. Very light. Heavy. Stir inside. Without your finger blushing.

En dehors, n'est-ce pas

pp Sur du velours jauni

Continuez

Plein de subtilité, si vous m'en croyez

Prominently, all right? On yellowed velvet. Continue. Full of subtlety, take my word for it.

Sans bruit, croyez-moi encore

Sec comme un coucou

pp ralentir (très)

en un souffle

2 Juin 1913

Noiselessly, believe me again. Dry as a cuckoo. Ritenuto. Rallentando (very). In a breath. June 2, 1913.

à Mademoiselle Claude Emma DEBUSSY

Nº 3 _ Españaña.

NO. 3: ESPAÑAÑA. Sort of Waltz. Under the pomegranate trees. Just like in Seville. Beautiful Carmen and the barber.

Climb up your fingers. Puerta Maillot. This fine fellow Rodríguez. Ritenuto. A tempo. Isn't it the alcade?

Pause. Plaza Clichy. Rue de Madrid. The cigar-factory girls.

à la disposicion de Usted

At your service. Diminuendo. Rallentando. August 25, 1913.

CHAPITRES TOURNÉS
EN TOUS SENS

à Robert MANUEL

Celle qui parle trop

CHAPTERS TURNED EVERY WHICH WAY. THE WOMAN WHO TALKS TOO MUCH. Lively. Legato. The poor husband shows signs of impatience. Let me talk. Listen to me. The poor husband (his theme). 8ᵛᵃ for the right hand only. I want a solid mahogany hat.

154

Madame Chose a un parapluie en os

Mademoiselle Machin épouse un homme qui est sec comme un coucou

Mrs. What's-her-name has a bone umbrella. Miss Whoozit is marrying a man who's dry as a cuckoo.

Ecoute-moi donc!

8ra pour la main droite seulement ....

ralentir

La concierge a mal dans les côtes

Le mari se meurt d'épuisement

Arrêt

Lent (très)

23 Août 1913

pp en un pauvre souffle

Now, listen to me! The concierge has an ache in her ribs. Rallentando. Pause. The husband dies of exhaustion. Slow (very). In a wretched breath. August 23, 1913.

à Monsieur Fernand DREYFUS

Le porteur de grosses pierres

He carries them on his back. His appearance is crafty
and full of certainty.

His strength amazes small children.

We watch him transporting an enormous rock
a hundred times larger than himself (it's pumice).

Il les porte sur le dos. Son air
est narquois et rempli de certitude.
Sa force étonne les petits enfants.
Nous le voyons alors qu'il trans-
porte une pierre énorme, cent fois
plus grosse que lui. *(c'est une pierre
ponce.)*

THE BEARER OF LARGE STONES. Very slowly. With a lot of effort. Wait. Painfully and by fits and starts. Dragging his legs.

Wait. He feels that the rock is slipping from his grasp: it's going to fall. Pause. That's done it!—It falls. August 25, 1913.

a Madame Claude DEBUSSY

Regrets des Enfermés *(Jonas et Latude)*

REGRETS OF THE IMMURED MEN (JONAH AND LATUDE [a historical prisoner in the Bastille]). Be moderate. They are seated in the shade. Come out. They reflect.

Plusieurs siècles les séparent

Jonas dit: Je suis le Latude marin

Latude dit: Je suis le Jonas français

They are several centuries apart in time. Apparent. Jonah says, "I am the Latude of the sea." Latude says, "I am the French Jonah."

Dehors

Cela sent le renfermé, d'après eux

Prominently. They think it smells stuffy. Somber.

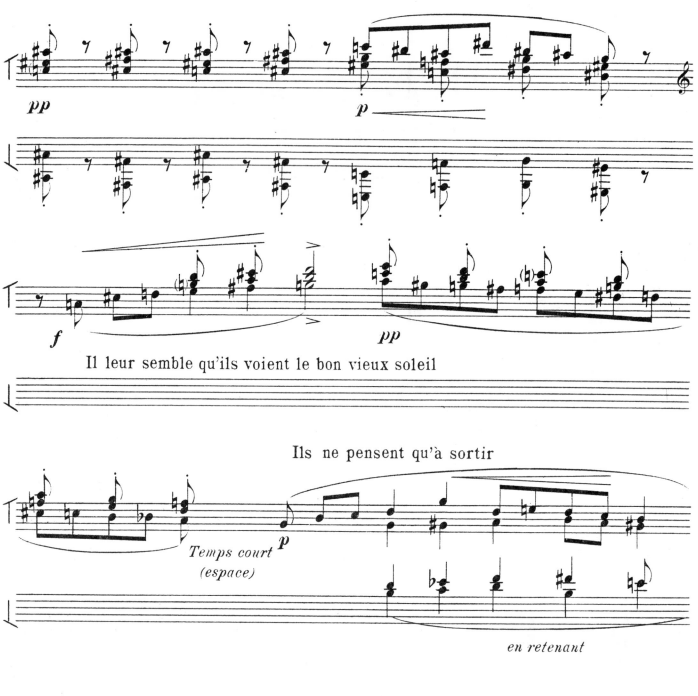

pp

p

f

Il leur semble qu'ils voient le bon vieux soleil

pp

Ils ne pensent qu'à sortir

Temps court *p*
(espace)

en retenant

Elargissez votre impression

f

ff

5 Septembre 1913

They think they see the good old sun. Brief pause (space). They think of nothing but getting out. Ritenuto. Broaden your impression.
September 5, 1913.

VIEUX SEQUINS ET VIEILLES CUIRASSES

à Ricardo VIÑES

I_ *Chez le Marchand d'or* *(Venise, XIIIᵉ Siècle)*

OLD SEQUINS AND OLD BREASTPLATES. I: AT THE GOLD MERCHANT'S (VENICE, 13TH CENTURY). Not too fast. He caresses his gold. He covers it with kisses.

Il embrasse un vieux sac

Il met dix mille francs d'or dans

sa bouche

Arrêt

Il prend une pièce d'or et lui parle à voix basse

He embraces an old sack. He puts 10,000 gold francs in his mouth. Pause. He takes a gold piece and talks to it quietly.

He acts like a child. He is happy as a king. He rolls into a chest, head downward.

Il en sort tout courbaturé

9 Septembre 1913

He comes out full of aches and pains. September 9, 1913.

à M.- D. CALVOCORESSI

II _ *Danse cuirassée* (*Période grecque*)

II: DANCE IN ARMOR (GREEK PERIOD). Noble military step. Moderato. Two rows of dancers.

Le premier rang ne bouge pas

Le second rang reste immobile

Ralentissez

Les danseurs reçoivent chacun un coup de sabre
qui leur fend la tête

17 Sept. 1913

The first row doesn't move. The second row remains stationary. Rallentando. Each dancer receives a saber blow that splits his head. Sept. 17, 1913.

à *Emile* **VUILLERMOZ**

III _ *La Défaite des Cimbres* (*Cauchemar*)

A very small child is sleeping in his very small bed. Every day his very aged grandfather gives him a kind of strange very small lesson in universal history, drawn from his vague memories.

He often tells him about the famous king Dagobert, the Duke of Marlborough and the great Roman general Marius.

In his dreams the very small child sees these heroes fighting the Cimbri at the battle of Mons-en-Puelle [near Lille] (1304).

Un tout petit enfant dort dans son tout petit lit. Son très vieux grand-père lui fait journellement une sorte d'étrange tout petit cours d'Histoire générale, puisée dans ses vagues souvenirs.

Souvent il lui parle du célèbre roi Dagobert, de Monsieur le Duc de Marlborough et du grand général romain Marius.

En rêve, le tout petit enfant voit ces heros combattant les Cimbres, à la journée de Mons-en-Puelle. (1304)

III. THE DEFEAT OF THE CIMBRI (NIGHTMARE). Without too much movement. Rain of javelins. Portrait of Marius.

Boïorix, roi des Cimbres

Boiorix, king of the Cimbri.

Il a du chagrin

p

pp

Les Dragons de Villars

f

Arrêt court *p*

pp

He is sorrowful. The dragoons of Villars [18th century]. Brief pause.

Le Sacre de Charles X (267bis)

Diminuendo. The coronation of Charles X [1825] (267bis). Grandiose. Ritenuto. Sept. 14, 1913.